For Paul and Ella   M.M.

Text by Christina Goodings
Illustrations copyright © 2008 Melanie Mitchell
This edition copyright © 2008 Lion Hudson

The moral rights of the author and illustrator
have been asserted

A Lion Children's Book
an imprint of
Lion Hudson plc
Wilkinson House, Jordan Hill Road,
Oxford OX2 8DR, England
www.lionhudson.com
UK ISBN: 978 0 7459 6087 6
US ISBN: 978 0 8254 7886 4

First edition 2008
This printing September 2009
10 9 8 7 6 5 4 3 2 1

A catalogue record for this book is available
from the British Library

Typeset in 36/40 Baskerville MT Schoolbook

Printed and bound in Singapore
by Tien Wah Press (Pte) Ltd

Distributed by:
UK: Marston Book Services Ltd, PO Box 269,
Abingdon, Oxon OX14 4YN
USA: Trafalgar Square Publishing, 814 N Franklin
Street, Chicago, IL 60610
USA Christian Market: Kregel Publications, PO Box
2607, Grand Rapids, MI 49501

See and Say!

Lost Sheep Story

Christina Goodings

Illustrated by Melanie Mitchell

LION
CHILDREN'S

The shepherd is counting.

One

two

three

baa baa

The shepherd is still counting.

A sheep is missing.
'I love my sheep,' he says.
'I must find it.'

Bye bye!

The shepherd is walking.

SSSSSS

Then the shepherd hears
a sound.

Hooray!

The shepherd goes home.
'I've found my lost sheep,'
he says.

baa baa

When someone who was lost is found, all the angels sing.

baa

la-la-la!